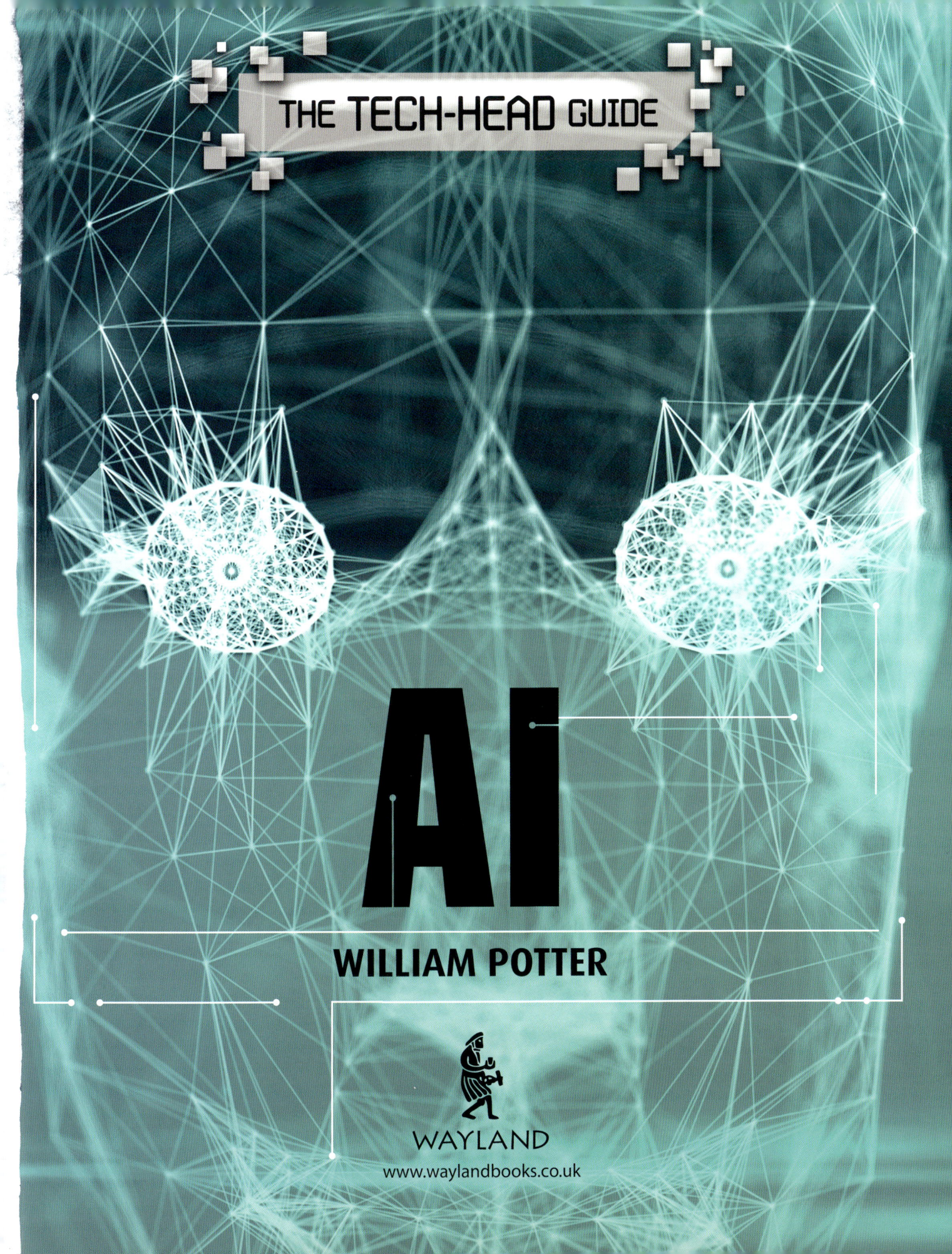

First published in Great Britain in 2020
by Wayland
Copyright © Hodder and Stoughton, 2020
All rights reserved
Editor: Elise Short
Designer concept: Wild Pixel Ltd
Designer: Jason Billin

HB ISBN: 978 1 5263 0985 3
PB ISBN: 978 1 5263 0986 0

Printed and bound in China

Wayland, an imprint of
Hachette Children's Group
Part of Hodder and Stoughton
Carmelite House
50 Victoria Embankment
London EC4Y 0DZ
An Hachette UK Company
www.hachette.co.uk
www.hachettechildrens.co.uk

The website addresses (URLs) included in this book were valid at the time of going to press. However, it is possible that contents or addresses may have changed since the publication of this book. No responsibility for any such changes can be accepted by either the author or the Publisher.

Picture credits:
Alamy: AF Archive/Disney2008 25tl; All Star Picture Library/Stanley Kubrick Production 1968 24cl; BSIP SA 19bl; dpa picture alliance 29tr; Media for Medical SARL 18r; Photo12/Disney 1982 24-25bg; Picture Luxe/The Hollywood Archive/Disney 2015 25bl; Science History Images 6bl; Science Photo Library 7tl. Tony Avelar/The Christian Monitor 20l. CAPTCHA 9cr. Chysler 13cl. Mike Cook/Games by Angelina.org 21c.DARPA 13tr.DoDAm systems bl back cover, 16bl. Nehemia Gershuni/Israeli Defence Forces 17b. Getty Images: Ilgan Sports/Multi-Bits 20-21bg; The Life Picture Collection 22bl. iRobot.co.uk 23bl. JPL/NASA 23br. JSC/NASA 27bl.Tim Kaulen/Carnegie Mellon University.Peter Menzel/SPL tr back cover, 22c. Microsoft research 11b. MIT 10l. Princetonai.com team: Eugene Demchenko, Sergey Ulasen, Selena Semoushkina, Mikhail Gershkovich, Vladimir Veselov, Laurent Alquier (graphics) 11t. RIKEN research centre br back cover, 26c. Shutterstock: front cover -Sergey Tarasov, Social Media Hub, icons 4-5b -Artfury , Rashad Ashur, Avicon , bhjary, Cube 29, dimorph, Fidart, grafixmania,, juli92, Kasue, Martial Red, suesse, Top Vector Stock, Ihor Zigor; agsandrew 28-29bg; Christoph Burgstedt 19t; Castleski 9t; Sergey Fatin 21b; Food Travel Stockforlife 18-19bg; garetsworkshop 8c; G_O_S 16-17bg; Kaspars Grinvalds 10r; Anton Gvozdikov 23t; Halfpoint 9cl; Sarah Holmlund 29bl; Immersion Imagery 1, 4-5 bg; jakkapan 22-23bg; Jenson 26b; Lee Jin-Man/AP/ Rex Features 14br; majcot 6-7bg, 30-31bg, 32bg; metamorworks 2-3 bg, 12-13bg, 12br; MSSA 14bl; Panuwatccn 27tl; Peshkova 26027bg; Andrey Popov 8-9bg, 8b; REDPIXEL 27tr; sdecoretn 28br; Tatiana Shepeleva 29br; SvedOliver 18l; Sergey Tarasov front cover; TierneyMJ 10-11bg; Vaalaa 17t; Lerner Vadim 5tr; Jan de Wild 5tl. Sense.ly 19cr. Stanford University 6cr. 343 Studio 14-15bg. US Navy Photo/PD/ MCS 3rd Class Gregory A Harden II 16-17c. Valve Corporation 15c. CC Wikimedia Commons/Lord Redthorn 7tr.

Every attempt has been made to clear copyright. Should there be any inadvertent omission please apply to the publisher for rectification.

CONTENTS

WHAT IS AI? 4
INTELLIGENCE TRAINING 6
GETTING TO KNOW YOU 8
AUTO ASSISTANTS 10
AUTONOMOUS AUTOS 12
GAME PLAYERS......................................14
MILITARY MIND 16
THE DOCTOR IS IN 18
ARTIFICIAL ARTISTS 20
AI AUTOMATONS 22
BIG-SCREEN BRAINS 24
AI TAKES OVER 26
ARTIFICIAL WORLD................................28
GLOSSARY / USEFUL SITES and BOOKS ..30
INDEX..32

WHAT IS AI?

There are many legends of human-made creations given intelligent life, from Frankenstein's monster to the earliest robots. Now fiction is becoming reality. Machines use artificial intelligence, or AI, to learn for themselves, figure out how to work better at their jobs, and make their own decisions. Now that's smart.

LEARNING TO LEARN

Early computer programs were designed to follow simple commands with predictable results. In the last half century, faster tech and access to the Internet have allowed for much more advanced programs that can gather information, test ideas and find the best solutions on their own. This human-like ability to learn is called **'artificial intelligence'** or **AI** for short.

CLEVER COMPUTING

Computer AI works by using sets of instructions called **algorithms**. These provide a series of steps to be followed to solve a problem, much as humans work out what to do. An algorithm for breakfast might be: find bowl, add cereal, pour milk on top, fetch spoon ...

TIMELINE

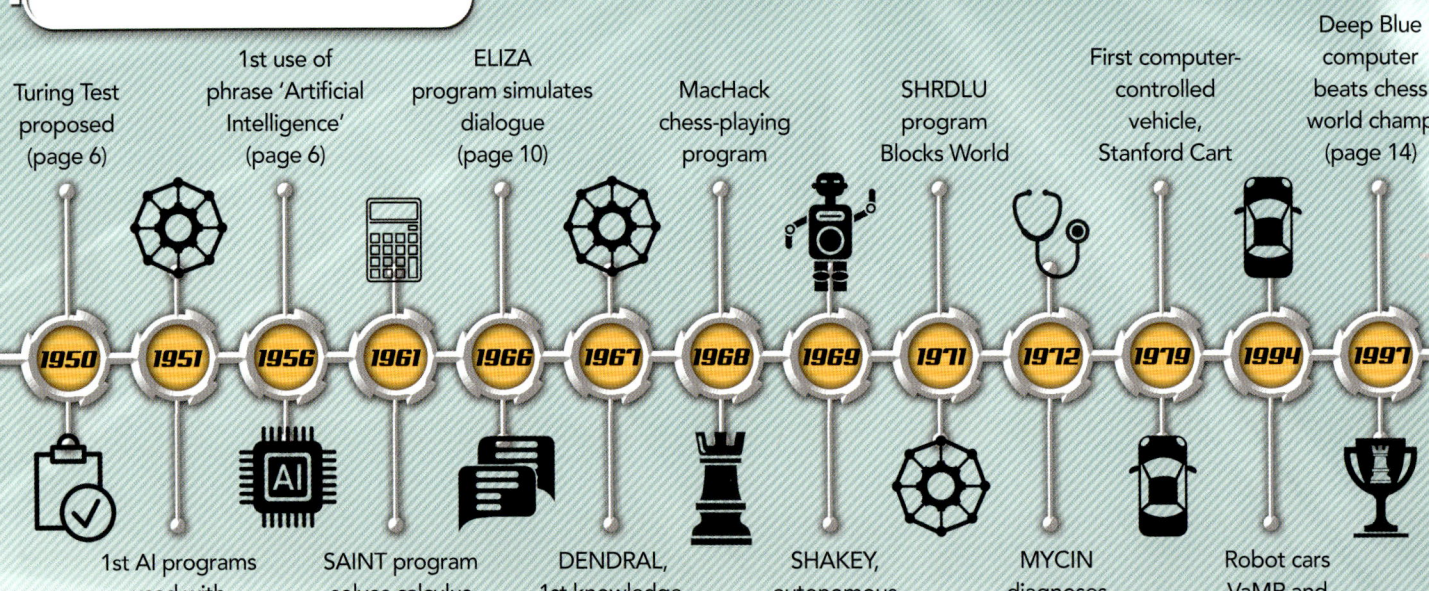

- **1950** — Turing Test proposed (page 6)
- **1951** — 1st AI programs used with Manchester Mark I
- **1956** — 1st use of phrase 'Artificial Intelligence' (page 6)
- **1961** — SAINT program solves calculus problems
- **1966** — ELIZA program simulates dialogue (page 10)
- **1967** — DENDRAL, 1st knowledge-based expert system (page 7)
- **1968** — MacHack chess-playing program
- **1969** — SHAKEY, autonomous robot is invented (page 23)
- **1971** — SHRDLU program Blocks World
- **1972** — MYCIN diagnoses infections (page 7)
- **1979** — First computer-controlled vehicle, Stanford Cart
- **1994** — Robot cars VaMP and VITA-2 drive 1,000 km in Paris
- **1997** — Deep Blue computer beats chess world champ (page 14)

4

SMART LIFE

Today, AI is all around us. It works in smartphones, **sat-nav** and **smart speakers**, for example by giving directions, recommending things to buy on the Internet and selecting a song playlist. AI controls characters in video games and can guide automatic vacuum cleaners, lawnmowers and self-driving cars. You may have been communicating with an AI program without knowing it, dealing with a **chatbot** instead of a human for online customer service.

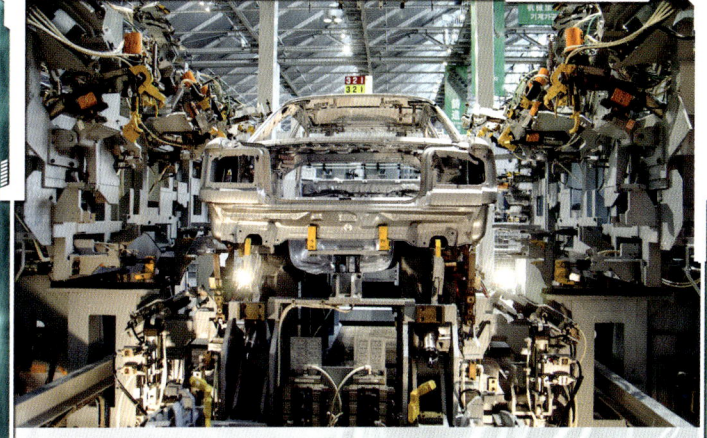

ROBOTS RULE

The AI in sci-fi films suggests people risk being replaced by intelligent machines. Is there a danger in giving machines the intelligence and freedom to adapt, improve and duplicate themselves? Or will artificial intelligence help free us from boring work, so we have more time for fun activities? Are you ready for an AI future? Read on to find out.

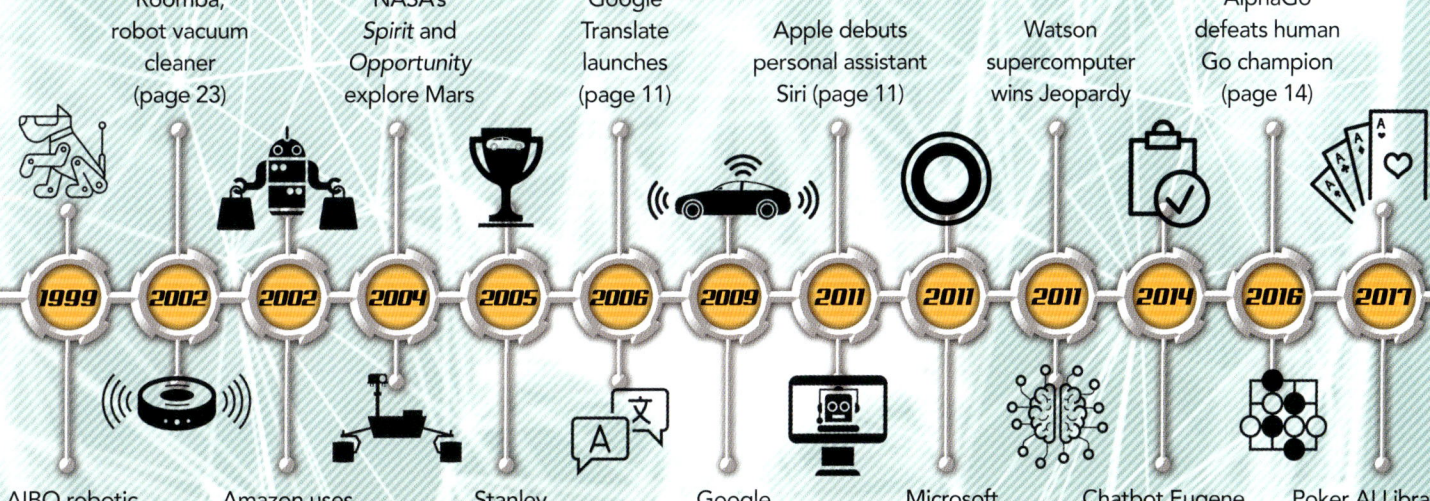

Roomba, robot vacuum cleaner (page 23)

NASA's *Spirit* and *Opportunity* explore Mars

Google Translate launches (page 11)

Apple debuts personal assistant Siri (page 11)

Watson supercomputer wins Jeopardy

AlphaGo defeats human Go champion (page 14)

1999 — 2002 — 2002 — 2004 — 2005 — 2006 — 2009 — 2011 — 2011 — 2011 — 2014 — 2016 — 2017

AIBO robotic pet goes on sale

Amazon uses automated product recommendation

Stanley wins DARPA challenge (page 13)

Google launches self-driving car

Microsoft launches Cortana

Chatbot Eugene Goostman passes Turing Test

Poker AI Libratus defeats four human opponents

5

INTELLIGENCE TRAINING

A computer program that could imitate human thinking was predicted in the 1950s. Since then, programmers have been designing more and more complex computer processors that work like our brain, gathering data from the Internet and taking lessons in a virtual world.

HUMAN OR MACHINE?

The British scientist **Alan Turing** helped develop technology to crack enemy codes during the Second World War (1939–45) and designed some of the first modern computers. In 1950 he suggested that it would be possible to create a machine that thought and communicated like a human. He developed a test, named the **Turing Test**, that could determine a machine's ability to 'think' and pass as human.

TECH TALK

The phrase **'Artificial Intelligence'** was first coined in 1955, by US scholar **John McCarthy**. He gathered a group of leading minds for a conference at Dartmouth College, New Hampshire to share ideas on using computers to replicate brain functions. This led to a boom in AI studies. McCarthy went on to create an AI programming language called **Lisp**, still in use today.

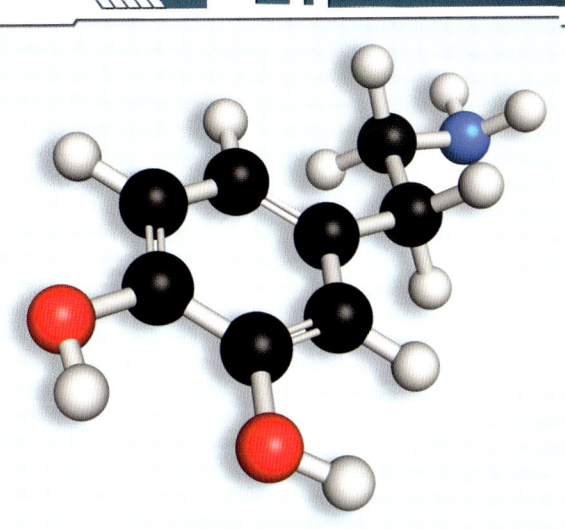

EXPERT HELP

Rather than create a computer program that does everything a human can, scientists chose to test AI with specific tasks. These **expert systems** were designed to recognise speech, play games or assist doctors. Early expert systems include **DENDRAL** (1965), which was taught to recognise chemicals, and **MYCIN** (1972), which diagnosed blood diseases.

KEEP ON CODING

The world's longest-lived AI project is **Cyc**. Since 1984, researcher Douglas Lenat and his team at **Cycorp** have been attempting to provide computers with all the common-sense knowledge of the average human, the kind of thing you can't just look up on the Internet. Typical facts on the Cyc database include "Every tree is a plant" and "Plants die eventually".

ELECTRONIC BRAIN

From the mid-1980s, with access to greater computing power, scientists developed microchips that work like the human brain. These **neural networks** use thousands or millions of connected artificial brain cells and have access to huge amounts of **data** from the Internet.

GETTING TO KNOW YOU

AI apps can be used to recognise faces and objects, helping security services to unlock devices such as smartphones and identify and track possible threats.

IMAGE SEARCH

Millions of images are uploaded to the Internet every day. To help you find the pictures you're looking for, search engines use sophisticated AI that can recognise people, animals and objects from the pattern of the pixels in pictures. The AI matches a search term, such as 'cats', with the best pictures. AI is also used to recognise and remove offensive content from websites.

AI EYES

Many airports now use **e-gates** at immigration controls. These automated border controls scan the faces of passengers and compare the images with the data on their **biometric** passports. Security services can track criminal suspects by matching images taken on CCTV camera with their databases from ID cards and driving licences. Artificial intelligence can compare images much quicker than humans can and alert police forces that a suspect has been spotted.

BEHAVE YOURSELF

AI can recognise behaviour as well as faces. Banks use AI to spot irregular transactions and alert users to potential credit-card misuse or uncover possible fraud. Internet shopping sites and supermarkets use AI to work out your preferences and recommend other items you might like to purchase.

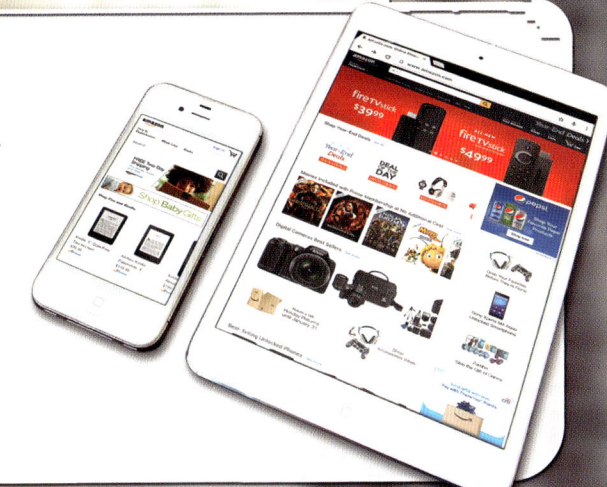

FACE KEY

These days, all you need to do to access a smartphone is to look at it. Apple's **Face ID** uses a **TrueDepth** infrared camera system to map the details of your face and assign it to your iPhone. To unlock the phone, you just need to glance at the screen, and the smartphone's chip matches it to an image on file. It can even recognise the same person under makeup, sunglasses, beards and in darkness.

I AM NOT A ROBOT

An AI is very good at identifying objects in images so long as it has had plenty of practice. They struggle much more in recognising a random object in a photo. To avoid computer programs auto-logging into websites, a program called **CAPTCHA** is sometimes used. CAPTCHA stands for 'Completely Automated Public Turing test to tell Computers and Humans Apart'. The system uses distorted text or a wide range of images that only humans can understand, and AIs are locked out.

AUTO ASSISTANTS

Say hi to AI! An important step in AI development was creating computer programs that could communicate in natural speech. 'Talking' to non-humans is now commonplace, with online assistants, customer services and chatbots answering our calls.

```
EEEEEEE  L         IIIIII  ZZZZZZZ    AAA
E        L           I           Z   A   A
EEEE     L           I          Z    A   A
E        L           I         Z     AAAAAA
E        L           I        Z      A   A
EEEEEEE  LLLLLLL   IIIIII    ZZZZZ   A   A

ELIZA > (PLEASE TYPE IN ALL CAPS) WHAT'S YOUR NAME DEAR ?
AMIT
ELIZA > HI. I'M ELIZA. WHAT DO YOU WANT TO TALK ABOUT ?
AMIT > CAN I TALK ABOUT MY PROBLEM ?
ELIZA > SURE... !
AMIT > DUE TO ON GOING EXAMS IN COLLEGE. I HAVE A LOT OF STRESS.
ELIZA > PLEASE RELAX A LITTLE. SLEEP WELL.
AMIT > THANKS FOR YOUR ADVICE.
ELIZA > NO MENTION.
AMIT > BYE
ELIZA > BYE AND KEEP IN TOUCH...
```

MEET ELIZA

Chatbots are computer programs that simulate everyday conversation. The first was introduced to the world in 1966 by **Joseph Weizenbaum**, a computer scientist from Massachusetts Institute of Technology (MIT) in Boston, USA. Named **ELIZA**, it was an early AI experiment in computer speech and was built to pass the Turing Test. ELIZA pretended to be a psychotherapist. It recognised phrases and gave replies designed to keep a chat going.

How can I help you?

• listening...

TEST SUBJECT

The first chatbot said to have passed the **Turing Test**, by convincing people it was a real person, was known as **Eugene Goostman**. Developed in Russia in 2001 by programmers Vladimir Veselov, Eugene Demchenko and Sergey Ulasen, Goostman was a program pretending to be a witty 13-year-old Ukrainian boy with a pet guinea pig. Goostman convinced a third of people chatting to it that it was a real young person.

VOICE CONTROL

Today, more and more people are using voice-control to access the Internet, through computers, smartphones and **smart speakers**. Virtual assistants such as Apple's **Siri**, Google's Assistant and Amazon's **Alexa** are interfaces that use **natural language processing** (NLP) to match spoken words to known commands. Typical commands include playing music or videos, shopping, checking the weather, or getting facts from online encyclopaedias.

WHO'S TALKING?

The voice at the end of the phone may sound human but it could be a chatbot using recordings of a real human voice to answer questions. Many banks, airlines and restaurants use automatic phone systems that can recognise numbers and phrases and lead you through a menu to access whichever services you need.

TRANSLATOR TECH

Google introduced its **Translate** program in 2006, using translated UN and European Parliament documents to gather data. Translate and Microsoft's Bing **Translator** now work with over 100 different languages using clever **neural machine translation** (NMT) to predict word sequences and translate whole sentences at a time.

In 2012, Microsoft research boss **Rick Rashid** impressed a Chinese audience by having his speech translated live from English to Chinese Mandarin, with his own speech patterns replicated. The hope is that one day people will be able to talk in any language using accurate translation tech.

AUTONOMOUS AUTOS

Would you trust a computer to drive you home? Self-driving, or autonomous cars are the future of road transport, taking passengers from A to B without the need for a human driver. Soon you could kick back, watch a film or even snooze while your AI gets behind the wheel.

GETTING AROUND

Self-driving cars work out where they are and where to go using **GPS** data that gets co-ordinates from orbiting satellites, just like a **sat-nav** device. For closer distances, they use cameras and a range of sensors, including radar and range-finding lasers **(LiDAR)**.

AI ASSIST

AI is already integrated in many modern cars that require human drivers. Computer programs help improve fuel and brake efficiency, give warnings and provide a cruise-control setting. Some cars even have an automatic parking system.

GRAND CHALLENGE

The **DARPA Grand Challenge** is an annual competition sponsored by the US Department of Defense to test **autonomous** vehicles on different tracks. The first car to pass the challenge was a driverless Volkswagen Toureg adapted by a team from Stanford University in 2005. The car, nicknamed **Stanley**, successfully steered its way around a 212 km desert course of winding mountain passes and tunnels in just under seven hours, winning the US$2 million prize.

TAKE A TOUR

Driverless cars are already running in some countries. In London's Heathrow Airport and Greenwich GATEway, four-seater driverless pods offer passengers the chance to experience driver-free travel, at careful slow speeds along special pathways. In the US, Google's **Waymo** are test-driving a fleet of self-driving taxis on public roads, while in Tokyo, Japan, robo-taxis are being successfully trialled. However the technology still needs improving, as a pedestrian was killed during a test in Arizona, USA in 2018.

AI INPUT
Name: Stanley
Vehicle Type: Volkswagen Toureg R5
Computer: 6 x 1.6 GHz Intel Pentium M
Average Speed: 30.7km/h

GAME PLAYERS

Computer programs are ahead of the game, having beaten human champions at chess and Go. AI also works behind the scenes in video games controlling the characters you play against.

CHESS CHAMP

Chess is one of the most difficult games to master. In 1997 the IBM computer **Deep Blue** took on the world chess champion **Garry Kasparov** and beat him in the first win of its kind. Deep Blue could consider 200 million chess positions every second to help it plan several moves ahead.

GO AHEAD

Another major win for a computer was a contest between Google's **DeepMind AlphaGo** and 18-time world champ Go player Lee Sedol in 2016. The Asian game **Go**, where players place counters to control sections of a board, is far more complex than chess. It requires intuition and creative thinking, not skills expected from machines, yet the AlphaGo won. It compared the moves in millions of previous games to outsmart Sedol.

WINNING HAND

Poker is a card game played with incomplete information – what cards do your opponents have? For every deal, there are 10^{161} (1 followed by 161 zeros) possible results. That's a figure greater than the total number of all the atoms in the universe! The AI **Libratus** was programmed by Professor Tuomas Sandholm to deal with this lack of data and compete with four top-class human players in a 20-day poker tournament in 2017. Libratus studied its opponents' style of play and changed its strategy to outwit them, storming to victory and winning a virtual US$1.7 million.

TEAMWORK

AIs can tackle video games too. **Dota 2** is a video game that requires players to work together to attack and destroy the other players' base. Developers at **OpenAI** trained five AIs to join forces and take on five human players in 2018. Racking up **180 years** of gameplay experience every day in the **Cloud**, they beat the human squad in two out of three matches. The human squad only just managed to win the third game.

THE NEXT LEVEL

Simple AI plays a part behind the scenes in video games such as *Halo*, *Metal Gear Solid* and *Far Cry*, controlling **non-player characters** (NPCs) to produce a limited number of actions. AI in games like *Nintendogs* persuades players that they can train virtual pets and alter their behaviour.

MILITARY MIND

AI is being used by the armed forces to guard borders and defend combat ships. The AI scans for threats and helps to target the right weapons. However, computer programs are not allowed to decide when to fire at – and kill – humans. That decision is always made by a human soldier.

BORDER CONTROL
The AI-controlled automated gun turret **Super aEgis II** is programmed to identify, track and destroy a moving target. Guarding borders in South Korea, the UAE and Qatar, the US$40 million piece of tech barks a command to 'Turn back or we will shoot!' when it spots a trespasser within range. While capable of firing on its own, the Super aEgis II is programmed only to fire with a password supplied by a human operator.

KILLER ROBOT CONTROL
AI-powered guns, planes, ships, planes and tanks are a real concern for many countries. The United Nations is supporting efforts to secure a ban on so-called 'killer robots', ensuring that "humans remain at all times in control over the use of force".

COMPUTER CANNON

Several navies, including the British and US, deploy the **Phalanx CIWS** anti-missile system aboard their combat ships as an automatic defence against attacks from enemy ships and helicopters. A computer controls a radar-guided 20 mm cannon to detect, track, engage and perform a 'kill assessment' to work out if a target can be successfully destroyed.

ROBO TANK

While self-driving cars are being introduced on public roads, the Russian army are working on AI-controlled tanks for the battlefield. With a digital control system and **autonomous** gun turret, the **T-14 Armata** could be the first step on the way to crewless tanks.

AIR SHIELD

Israel uses a mobile all-weather air defence system called **'Iron Dome'** to protect itself from air attack. The AI-controlled system has so far intercepted and destroyed a reported thousand rockets aimed at populated areas. The Iron Dome system uses radar to track rockets and advanced software to predict the missile's flight path. Iron Dome can currently protect a 70 km area.

AI INPUT

Name: Phalanx CIWS
Type: Close-in weapon station
Manufacturer: General Dynamics
Guidance System: Radar, infrared
Firing Range: 3.5 km

THE DOCTOR IS IN

Computer programs are becoming an essential aid in healthcare, able to check millions of medical histories in seconds and even providing help in the operating theatre. Meet the AI doctor.

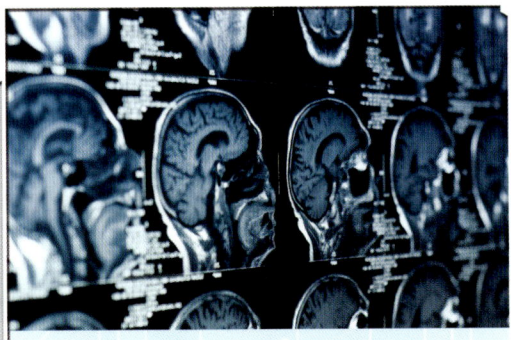

SPEED SCANS

To make a diagnosis, a doctor may need to consult several scans of a patient, such as ultrasound, MRI scans and X-rays. Comparing results can be time-consuming. Training a computer to recognise signs of injury or illness, such as cancer, in scans can save time and lives. This is the perfect job for AI.

CUTTING EDGE

How safe would you feel facing a robot surgeon? Computer-assisted surgery is already in use. The **da Vinci** system is controlled by a human surgeon through a console with a magnified view. The surgeon's hand gestures can be translated into tiny, precise movements by the robotic instruments, meaning smaller, neater incisions and a quicker recovery for patients. For now, AI is used as an assistant in the operating room but fully automated surgeons for routine operations are sure to follow.

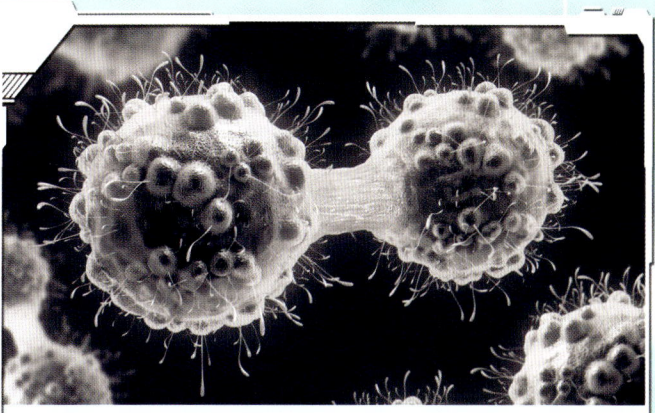

A CURE FOR CANCER

Software giant **Microsoft** is investing in healthcare technology. Their **Project Hanover** initiative aims to use **machine learning** to gather information on new cancer drugs and results to help doctors choose the right course for future patients. **IBM** have a similar AI program, named **Watson**, which sifts through millions of medical records to find the best treatments.

Please tell me your main symptom.

VIRTUAL NURSE

Imagine a nurse who is available 24/7 to check on your health and offer advice. Meet **Angel**, the first AI nurse assistant. This bot deals with patients over the phone, providing advice, reminders and arranging appointments. Virtual nurses and apps provide support for patients and save time for human medical staff.

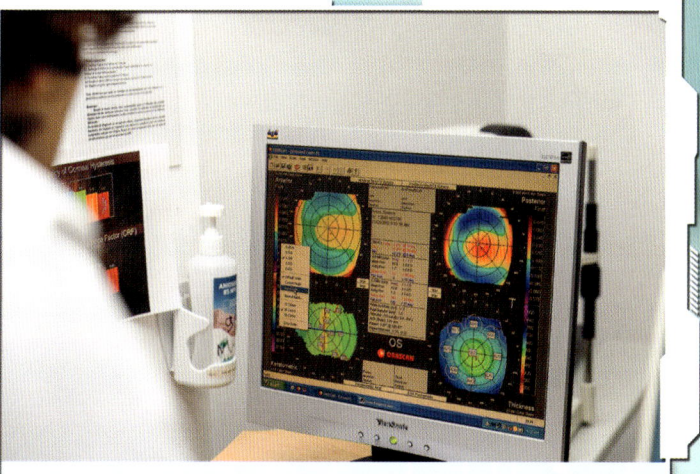

IN SIGHT

Machines are just as good as humans at detecting eye problems. Google's **DeepMind** has been working with the UK's Moorfields Eye Hospital to develop an AI that can check patients' retina scans and detect signs of 50 different eye diseases that need treatment.

ARTIFICIAL ARTISTS

Could an AI create great art, music, games or stories? Programmers are testing the idea of computational creativity with amazing results.

COMPUTER COMPOSERS

In 1981 professor **David Cope** was struggling to write the music for an opera when he decided to use a computer for help, programming it to mimic his musical style. His **Experiments in Musical Intelligence**, or **Emmy**, for short was then developed to write in the style of composers, such as Mozart and Bach. A new version of the musical AI went on to release a CD in 2010 under the name **Emily Howell**.

PROGRAMMED POP

It's not only in the classical world that AI is tuning up. It's ready to take the pop world by storm. Companies such as **Jukedeck** allow users to select a musical style, mood and speed before an AI generates an original tune. South Korean girl group Spica (pictured) is just one of several K-Pop acts that have used the tech to invent melodies for their songs.

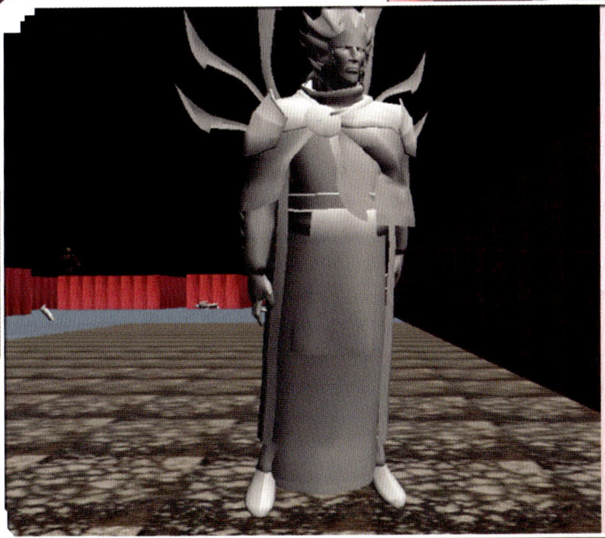

GAME CONTROLLER

If AI is good at adding characters to video games, why not have one invent its own game? That's the idea behind **Angelina**. The brainchild of AI researcher Mike Cook, Angelina comes up with the rules of a game, gets inspiration and images from the Internet and delivers new surreal game experiences.

TECH WITH TASTE

Computers are also cooking up something in the kitchen. IBM's **Chef Watson** AI uses a database of food knowledge, including the chemical composition of different ingredients, to invent new dishes for chefs to serve up. Here are some favourites:

Creole Shrimp-Lamb Dumpling
Austrian Chocolate Burrito
Hoof-and-Honey Ale
Strawberry Curry

Chef Watson even has its own cookbook.

AI AUTOMATONS

AI is on the move, controlling robots that can get to know their environment, can pick up and move objects, help around the house and even meet and greet humans.

SHAKEY START

SHAKEY could be considered the first mobile, autonomous robot. Built in the late 1960s by researchers at the Stanford Research Institute, USA, SHAKEY could find its way across a room by pushing obstacles out of the way. Because computers were huge at that time, the robot had to be connected to one via a radio link.

EMOTIONAL FEEDBACK

Kismet was a rather freaky-looking robot head built by Massachusetts Institute of Technology (MIT) in 1997. It could recognise the way humans spoke and observe body language, then reply with facial expressions and a simulated emotional voice.

MEDIA STAR

Sophia is an advanced robot designed by Hong Kong's Hanson Robotics. Activated in 2015, she is already a Facebook star and has appeared on prime-time TV and the cover of a fashion magazine. Her AI helps improve the way she reacts to people by adapting the sound of her voice, developing a sense of humour, and using different hand gestures and one of 50 facial expressions.

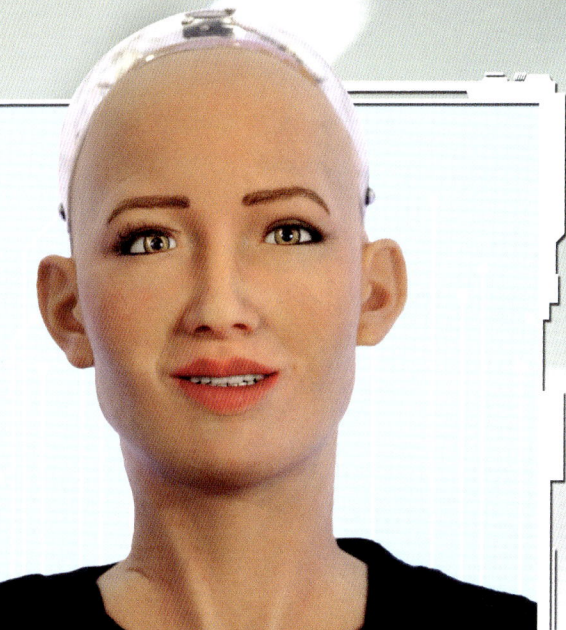

CLEANING UP

Cleaning robots have been a dream for decades. While appearing quite simple, **iRobot's Roomba** is a smart vacuum cleaner that uses sensors to guide its way across carpets and floors and around furniture, brushing and sucking up dirt. Its AI works out the best route and automatically returns the robot to its charging base after completing the job.

MARS TECH

Possibly the most impressive autonomous robot is the one that is making decisions 55 million km away from its human designers. Since 2012, NASA's **Curiosity** rover has been rolling across the planet Mars using AI called **AEGIS.** This system uses a laser detection system to identify rocks worth investigating. Part of its mission is to find out if Mars could once have supported life.

BIG-SCREEN BRAINS

Sci-fi books and films have been predicting the rise of AI for decades, not always in a positive way. What can we learn about AI from these stories?

TAKEOVER

In the 1968 film **2001: A Space Odyssey, HAL 9000** is the computer controlling the *Discovery One* on a mission to Jupiter. When the ship's crew suspect HAL of making mistakes, it kills them one by one before it can be shut down and stopped from completing its mission.

TRON

Made in 1982, **Tron** was one of the first films to feature computer-generated imagery. It follows the adventures of a programmer who is digitised and downloaded into a deadly computer game controlled by a powerful AI.

JUNK PLANET

In the future of 2008's computer-animated film **WALL-E**, a lone robot AI is left to clean up a polluted Earth while humanity has been sent into space on starships controlled by an AI. When the Earth is found to be habitable again, the AI refuses to steer the ships back home.

INFLATABLE FRIEND

The computer-animated 2014 film **Big Hero 6** features a teenage robotics genius called Hiro and an inflatable healthcare robot AI called Baymax. Together with a small group of heroes they track down the tech corporation responsible for the death of Hiro's brother.

THE NEXT STEP

Here are more films featuring amazing AI that you can watch at a suitable age:

- The *Terminator* films (1984–2019) feature an AI defence system that attempts to rid Earth of humanity using lethal androids.
- *A.I.* (2001) stars David, an abandoned android in the form of a young boy, who tries to locate a family.
- *The Matrix* trilogy (1999–2003) shows humans being used as living batteries by machines while they live in a virtual reality.
- *Ex Machina* (2014) features a programmer invited to test Ava, an advanced android who uses her intelligence to escape into the wider world.
- *Avengers: Age of Ultron* (2015) has an AI, in an almost indestructible metal body, take on the Avengers with his android army.

25

AI TAKES OVER

A future with AI does not necessarily mean being ruled by an army of androids. There are many benefits to having a program take over some human tasks.

NURSE BOT
AI is already supplying health advice via apps, and assisting doctors with robotic surgeons. The next step could be artificially intelligent nurses providing medication. Faced with an ageing population, robot home-help may be a solution to keeping older people independent.

NEW SKILLS
The downside to robots doing jobs is when they replace human staff who cannot find new work. Self-driving vehicles could replace human taxi and truck drivers. AIs could take the jobs of assembly workers and financial analysts. But there will be new jobs for the new age, such as AI trainers, plus creative skills will be in even higher demand.

FREE TIME
With legions of robots helping out and doing dangerous or repetitive jobs, human workers could have more time for leisure and being creative. Maybe they will spend the time with an entertainment AI!

INVESTOR INTEL

Nowadays, most business is done online. AI can provide passwords and check for fraud, but it can also help work out the best money deals. In the near future, you can sit back and watch your funds grow while a computer program invests on your behalf.

SMART HOMES

Many household appliances can now link up online. With the **Internet of Things**, smart fridges know when you're low on milk or other groceries and add them to your online shopping list for the next delivery. Soon devices could automatically update or even request repairs and spare parts without you being involved, and your alarm clock could wake you early when it finds out about delays on your work journey.

ROBONAUTS

Without the need for air, food or water, AIs could become artificial astronauts and explore the further reaches of the Solar System and beyond – journeys that are far too long for people to consider. NASA's **R5 Valkyrie** robonaut is already being developed to help out on a potential Mars mission.

ARTIFICIAL WORLD

Scientists talk of a moment called the Singularity when AI becomes smarter than the human mind and overtakes us leading to even faster progress and changes. What would that mean for our future with machines?

MEGA UPGRADES
With AI able to upgrade itself without human programmers, it could improve at faster and faster rates, becoming something we could never outsmart – a superintelligence.

AI IN CONTROL
Once AI becomes smarter than us, what role will it take? We could use AI to run the world more efficiently than us, but how much responsibility would we trust to a computer that has no feelings? Will AI be our clever helper, improving our lives, or will it become our master?

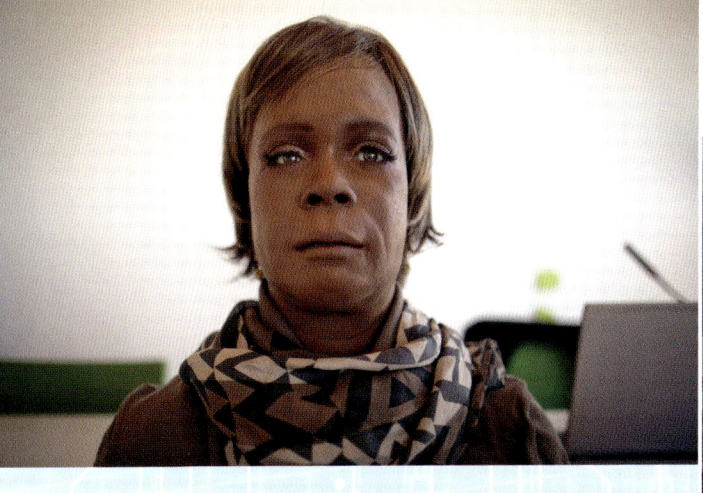

MEMORY MACHINES

Will knowledge of the human brain improve so far that your memory and personality could be uploaded to a computer program as a back-up? Hanson Robotics are testing this idea by programming the animated robot **BINA48** with the memories, beliefs and mannerisms of a woman named Bina Aspen. In the future, could we continue to talk to friends and family after their deaths as the human race lives on in machines?

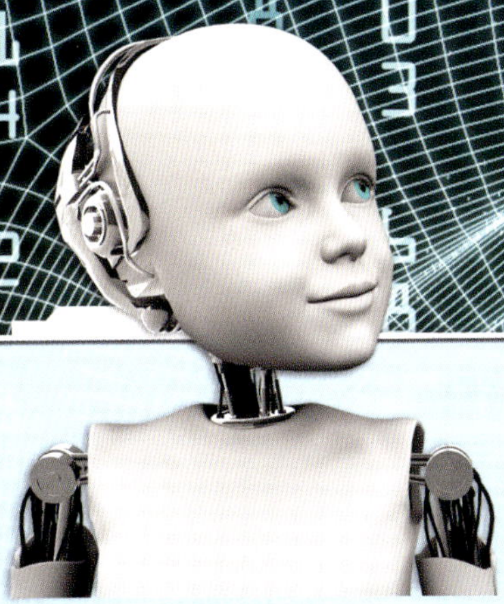

AI RIGHTS

As AIs get smarter, and learn and react just as humans do, with opinions and personality, would we have to accept them as living beings with the same rights as us? How about having an AI brother, sister or best friend?

HALF-MACHINE

Transhumanism is the idea that people can evolve through the use of science and tech. Bionic implants are already possible, with mechanical eye, hand and heart replacements. Could the next step be a merging of human and machine, with 3D-printed bones and super-intelligent AI assisting the human brain?

GLOSSARY

Algorithm Set of rules to be followed to work out the solution to a problem

Autonomous Free to control itself

Big Data Large amounts of information that can be use to work out trends and patterns

Biometric Personal statistics saved on a computer chip for identification purposes

Chatbot Computer program designed to have conversations with humans

Cloud Computer servers connected over the Internet

DARPA A US military research group, stands for the 'Defense Advanced Research Projects Agency'

Database Organised set of information in a computer

Expert systems Software that uses expert knowledge to provide answers

GPS Global Positioning System that uses satellite signals to work out location

Internet of Things Network of devices that can communicate with each other

LiDAR Detection system that reflects lasers to sense what is ahead

Natural Language Processing (NLP) Computer use of language, such as English, to receive commands

Neural Machine Translation (NMT) Translation program that uses the neural network to predict word sequences

Neural networks A computer system modelled on the human brain and nervous system

Non-player characters (NPCs) Background characters in a video game

Pixel The smallest unit of an image on a television or computer screen

Sat-Nav Navigation using info from orbiting satellites

Singularity The moment at which AI becomes smarter than people

Smart speaker Internet-connected device that can understand spoken commands and provide answers

Transhumanism Possible step in human evolution – human plus machine

Turing Test Test to show machine behaviour like that of a human

Virtual Reality Computer-generated 3D environment

USEFUL SITES

Google AI
Google's AI development: ai.google

Google AI Experiments
Showcase for machine learning experiments: google.com/collection/ai

The Painting Fool
Computer program painter: thepaintingfool.com

Sophia the Robot
Facebook page for Sophia the robot: facebook.com/realsophiarobot

USEFUL BOOKS

Machines That Think, New Scientist (John Murray)

The Story of Computing, Dermot Turing (Arcturus)

Artificial Intelligence, Richard Urwin (Arcturus)

Artificial Intelligence, Michael Wooldridge (Ladybird)

64 Things You Need to Know Now for Then, Ben Hammersley (Hodder & Stoughton)

INDEX

A
AI
    and cars 5, 12–13
    and composing music 20
    and creativity 20–21
    and games/gaming 5, 7, 14–15, 21
    and medicine 4, 7, 18–19, 26
    and robots (see robots)
    and the armed forces 16–17
    and translation 11
    in films 24–25
Alexa (Amazon) 11
Apple
    Face ID 9
    Siri 5, 11
assistants, online 10–11
automatons (see robots)

C
CAPTCHA 9
cars,
    autonomous 12–13
    driverless 13
    self-driving 4–5, 12–13, 17
    Stanley 5, 13
chatbots 5, 10–11, 19
chess 4, 14
Cook, Mike 21
Cope, David 20
Cyc 7

D
DARPA Grand Challenge 5, 13
defence, air 17
DENDRAL 4, 7

E
ELIZA 4, 10

G
Go (game) 5, 14
Google
    AlphaGo 5, 14
    Assistant 11
    DeepMind 14, 19
    self-driving cars 5
    Translate 5, 11
    Waymo 13
Goostman, Eugene 5, 11
guns, AI 16–17
    Phalanx CIWS 17
    Super aEgis II 16

I
IBM
    Chef Watson 21
    Deep Blue 4, 14
    Watson 5, 19
Internet of Things 27

K
Kasparov, Gary 14

L
Lenat, Douglas 7
Libratus 5, 15
Lisp 6

M
McCarthy, John 6
Microsoft 5
    Bing Translator 11
    Project Hanover 19
MYCIN 4, 7

N
NASA 5, 23, 27
nurses, virtual 19

P
passports, biometric 8
poker 5, 15
processing, natural language 11

R
Rashid, Rick 11
recognition, facial 8–9
robots
    BINA48 29
    Curiosity rover 23
    da Vinci surgery system 18
    future robots 26–27
    Kismet 22
    robonauts 27
    R5 Valkyrie 27
    Roomba 5, 23
    SHAKEY 4, 22
    Sophia 23
rovers, Mars 5, 23

S
Sandholm, Professor Tuomas 15
scans, medical 18–19
Second World War 6
Sedol, Lee 14
Singularity, the 28–29
space 5, 23
Spica 20

T
tanks, crewless 17
transhumanism 29
Turing, Alan 6
Turing Test 4–6, 9–11

W
Weizenbaum, Joseph 10

THE TECH-HEAD GUIDE

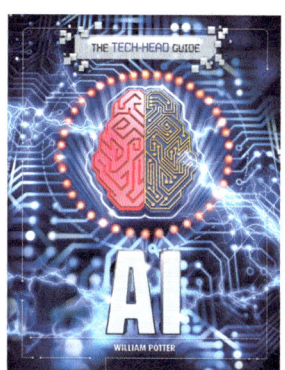

What is AI? • Intelligence training • Getting to know you • Auto assistants • Autonomous autos • Game players • Military mind • The doctor is in • Artificial artists • AI automatons • Big-screen brains • AI takes over • Artificial world • Glossary / Useful sites and books • Index

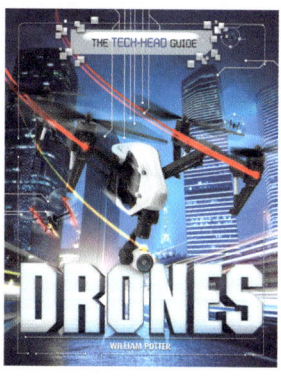

What is a drone? • History of the drone • Anatomy of a drone • Under control • Delivery drones • Mapping the world • Military drones • Eye in the sky • To the rescue • The race is on • All-stars • The war on drones • Into the future • Glossary / Useful sites and books • Index

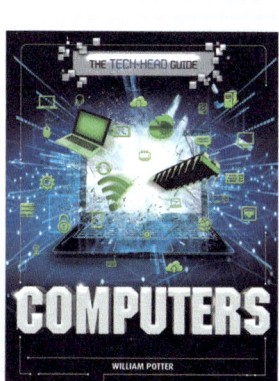

Computer world • History of the computer • Let's get personal • Inside the box • Software secrets • Digital data • Connected • Creative code • Under attack • Stay safe • Game on • Cyber cool • The next level • Glossary / Useful sites and books • Index

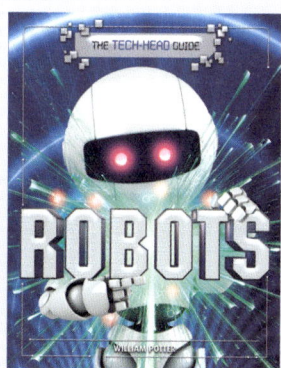

Robots rule! • Age of the automaton • Robots for real • Build a bot • Danger droids • Mobile machines • Battlefield bots • Auto industry • Robot replacements • Awesome androids • Mechanical megastars • Electric dreams • The next upgrade • Glossary / Useful sites and books • Index